Spiritual Journey:

LIFE'S ETERNAL BLESSINGS

Ann Marie Ruby

DEDICATION

I dedicate this book to all of whom do not have a family and are looking for a family. Please consider me your spiritual family. I believe as long as there is a spiritually awakened soul in this universe, we are a family. I am your family as you are mine. I shall always be there for all spiritually awakened souls. May we spread peace as we find peace. Like I always say, "Spread peace, be in peace."

INTRODUCTION

Words are my life's eternal blessings. Even when they hurt, I know I must stand up and fight for the truth, but always with words of blessings, not with curses. I believe words left out, always remain out there forever.

As words came towards me like a windstorm, I knew at times that they almost knocked me down. The unfelt, unknown, invited or uninvited, powerful stranger called words just comes and leaves behind love, joy, and pain. So, I have taken words as my friend and have written my books with words of love and blessings for all of whom are searching for a friend who is known by the name Words.

I have also written a very special book of 100 original prayers, as well as books of inspirational quotations from my soul. The story of my life is how I kept all of my work in my chest as a sacred spiritual journey. Never had I wanted to publish, but I kept them in my chest as a gift for all of whom ask, seek, or knock for them. I have seen there are so many people who need a friend called words of hope, inspiration, and prayers.

I have seen dreams in which I knew I must write to inspire all and maybe my writing can be the inner strength to awaken you spiritually for yourself.

I have decided to come out from my sacred cave and give these words as a gift for all of whom but want a friend as they too are taking a sacred journey through life. Hold on to this friend as you journey through life in your own way, in your own time. May these inspirational quotations be there for you as you need a friend through the journey of life.

From my soul, I give you these simple words of inspiration,
I call *Spiritual Journey: Life's Eternal Blessings.*

JOURNEY OF MY LIFE

My Lord,

My Creator,

You have but placed us, the travelers,

Upon this journey,

With struggles, agony, pain, health, wealth,

Wisdom, love, and victory

As our companions of life.

May I, Your devotee, the traveler,

Have as my companion only Your blessings

As I embark upon this blessed

JOURNEY OF MY LIFE.

*From my prayer book, *Spiritual Songs: Letters From My Chest*.

"*Life* is a blessed *journey*, where we have *endurance* as our *support*."

Quotation #1

"*Focus* on the
complete truth only,
as it is *found*
within each *soul*."

Quotation #2

"*Security* resides within our *soul*. As we *share* amongst all, it is *then* security is *found*."

Quotation #3

"*Starvation* from food kills the *human body*, as starvation from *knowledge* kills *the* mind, body, and *soul*."

Quotation #4

"*Humanity* is under attack as *humans roam* the lands without *it*."

Quotation #5

"*Plant* the seeds of *love* within your *soul*. Watch them *grow* as the *sun* shines through the *hearts* and the *rain* pours *through* the *teardrops*."

Quotation #6

"*Love* pours through as the *ocean touches* the lands *creating* this beautiful *Earth*."

Quotation #7

"*Angels* roam around all over this *Earth*. Open your *doors* to *find* them at your *doorstep*."

Quotation #8

"*When* blessings but knock on our *door* like strangers, *may* we but *greet* them and not send *them* away thinking, *oh* but *strangers*."

Quotation #9

"*Strangers*, strange lands, strange *words*, become *related through* the simple *word* known as *love*."

Quotation #10

"*The* path of life is *entwined* with *complications* and *love.*"

Quotation #11

"*Tears* we share for the *strangers* are our *sacred* journey as they *cleanse* the *soul* from within. May these *tears* be *our* awakened spiritual *souls*."

Quotation #12

"*Love* is the greatest *warrior* of all time as the sweet *tune* he sings for all *is* his true *soulmate*."

Quotation #13

"*Crossroads* and *obstacles* only warn us of the red *danger* in *front* of us, so be *steady* for then *we* shall be green to *go*."

Quotation #14

"*Human* vehicles are bonded to Earth *and* carry *Earthly* burdens. *Spiritual* vehicles set us *free* from all *bondages*."

Quotation #15

"*Mountain* spring *washes* the *Earthly* vehicle. *Inner* rejuvenation cleanses the *soul*."

Quotation #16

"*Tools* are
to be *handled* with
caution. The most
powerful tool in
this *universe* is the
mind. Use it
wisely."

Quotation #17

"*Love* heals all
as it *wipes* away
the *wounds* also
caused by *love*."

Quotation #18

"*A* mystery book is only a *mystery* until it is *read*. *Take* the effort and *open* the *pages*."

Quotation #19

"*Endurance* tests *herself* through the *struggles* of life. As she *succeeds*, her *name* changes to *endured*."

Quotation #20

"*Life* gives birth to *obstacles* and *endurance*. As they *begin* to battle *amongst themselves*, we *hold* on to *patience*."

Quotation #21

"*Weather* changes faces as she *travels* through *life*. Do not *fall* prey. Know her *actions* before she *arrives*."

Quotation #22

"'*Weather* can be a *friend* in disguise as long as *you* are *prepared* for her,' say the *wise*."

Quotation #23

"*From* amongst the dark clouds *hiding* behind the *fog*, *pouring* like a *glimpse* of hope, the biggest star the *sun* but *appears*."

Quotation #24

"*Life's* never-ending *obstacles* appear and *disappear* as we *learn* to walk through *life.*"

Quotation #25

"*Holding* on to the glimpse of *hope*, one but *spreads* hope *throughout eternity.*"

Quotation #26

26

"*Hold* on to the glimpse of *hope* for dawn *breaks* open *through* the dark night's *sky*."

Quotation #27

"*Memories* made, pull us *backwards*, when we *must* walk *forward* towards *making* more *memories*."

Quotation #28

"*Waiting* for the
achievements is
the only *way*
the *achiever* but
achieves."

Quotation #29

"*Humor* awakens
the human *mind*
to be just *human*."

Quotation #30

"*Life* turns around at all obstacles and wants help from within the soul. The soul then guides all through dreams. Awaken yourself and live life's eternal dreams. As all obstacles are overcome, life completes the blessed *dreams*."

Quotation #31

"*Treasure* life from within your *chest*, for even when *life* is no *more*, the *treasures* from within your *chest* live on for *eternity*."

Quotation #32

"*House*
is but just *walls*
keeping a *family*.
Heart is a home
for *all* throughout
eternity."

Quotation #33

"*Apologies* are but *words*. *Forgiveness* is *mercy*. Apologize, *forgive*, then be the *mercy*."

Quotation #34

"*The* human mind and *body* fight to *survive* each day as the spiritual *soul* fights *to* be awakened *from* within the *body*. As this journey is *completed*, the mind, body, *and* soul are but *united*."

Quotation #35

"*No* need to climb the *mountains* to find *peace* for peace is but within each *soul*."

Quotation #36

"*Human* body feasts within *Earthly* desires, *yet* the spiritual soul *desires* only *freedom*."

Quotation #37

"*Journey* life *through* the struggles of the *past* travelers, as *they* have *conquered* the *obstacles* and left *behind* the *guidelines* from their *journey*."

Quotation #38

"*Life* claims no *victory*, but only *teaches* for victory, for *life* is the *teacher*."

Quotation #39

"*Teachers* are the *students* of life, always *learning* to be the *learned.*"

Quotation #40

"*Difference* between the *learning* and the *learned* is the simple story of *life*."

Quotation #41

"*Faith* is the *unknown*, unseen, unheard *face* of complete *trust*."

Quotation #42

"*Difference* between *what* is *found* and *what* is not found but *believed*, is *called* the complete *faith*."

Quotation #43

"*Love* withstands the *windstorms* of *history*, for even with *time* passing us by, *love* lives on for *eternity*."

Quotation #44

"*Vacation* from *negativity* is *awakening* the spiritual *soul*, so set your soul *free* as you *take* a *vacation* from all *negativity*."

Quotation #45

"*Stand* up and walk for yourself. *Never* let another *walk* all over *you*."

Quotation #46

"*Claiming* to know but everything *cuts* your *knowledge* as *then* you but have *nothing* more to *learn*."

Quotation #47

"*Close* your eyes *when* a thorn but comes towards *you*, but do *remember* to open your *eyes* to *catch* the *blessings*."

Quotation #48

"*Keep* the lantern glowing all *night* so the lost *souls* find their way back. *With* each *household* *glowing* one after another, *there* will be no lost *souls*."

Quotation #49

"*The* ocean, the *mountain*, and the trees *share* the same Mother *Earth*. May we learn from *them* and *share* her in *union* amongst all *humans*."

Quotation #50

"*Memories* cross
time to be *made*.
May *we* leave
them *behind* with
love."

Quotation #51

"*Criticizing* a grown-up is *easy*, but *let* us get back to the *present* and hold on *to* each *child* so they do not go *astray*. Then, in the *future*, there shall be no *criticism*."

Quotation #52

"*May* we, the present, spread *peace* amongst *ourselves* so when the *future* but lands upon our *door*, we shall *all* be in *peace*."

Quotation #53

"*May* we, the present, sow the *seed* of peace all *around* us, for as the trees but *grow* up, it is *then*, they shall *protect* us from the *rain*, the sun, and be the *bearer* of *peace*."

Quotation #54

"*Cleanse* the mind, body, and *soul* from *within*, for then you *shall* be *blessed* with *the* pure essence of *cleanliness*."

Quotation #55

"*Life* lives on forever as *through* the *tunnels* of memories, *the* past, present, *and* future but become an *album* of *life*."

Quotation #56

"*Messages* travel *time*, so keep them in your *chest* with care, *for* in due *time*, all humans become the *time travelers* through the *messages*."

Quotation #57

"*Hold* on to the *positivity* for when time is *over*, let this action *travel* to the *future* spreading *positivity* throughout *time*."

Quotation #58

"*Pick* up all of your *hidden* mess for if not then, as *you* travel time to the *future*, your mess *will* be left *behind* for the next *generation* to *clean* up after *you*."

Quotation #59

"*Time* travelers *are* but all *humans* for as the *future* becomes the *present*, the present becomes the *past*."

Quotation #60

"*Hope* is not seen or felt, but is *spread* by you for *another*. Hope *comes* and *knocks* on your *door* as she is spread by you *first*."

"*Peace* comes after you have *taken* the time to *gently* lay her down like a *blanket* amongst *all*. It is then, she *finds* her way back to *comfort* your *heart*."

Quotation #62

"*Words* are the *blanket* of wisdom during the *cold* winter's *night*, as they spread *warmth* from house to *house*."

Quotation #63

"*Life* is a journey where words are our lifetime companions. We leave them in love and anger, with or without care; however, as they are left behind, they become our footprints for the future *generation*."

Quotation #64

"*Nothing* is but lost *and* nothing is but *found*. The only thing that *remains throughout eternity* is but *hope*. Hold on to *it*."

Quotation #65

"*Dancing* throughout *the* winter *and* summer storms, *nature* teaches *us* her anger *and* fury, and *buries* all her *differences* as she *plants* the flowers of *love*."

Quotation #66

"*Mother* sky buries all her *tears* throughout *the* clouds. As the *pain* strikes her, she *pours* them hard *onto* the *Earth* and from her tears, *we* the *children* clench our *thirst*."

Quotation #67

"*The* truth is but *hidden* under the *mountain* and with time, *all* shall be *found* as the *mountain* but erupts and *spreads* all the hidden *truth.*"

Quotation #68

"*Searching* for the unknown but *holds* us a *prisoner* in the land of the *lost*. Let the *words* of the *wise* guide us to *find* the known first, then the *unknown* but becomes *known*."

Quotation #69

"*Love* finds its way back *through* the *tunnels* of rebirth. It is then, the mind, body, *and* soul *awaken spiritually.*"

Quotation #70

"*Free* spirit
finds the free soul. It
is our mind and body
that capture us
as prisoners
from spiritually
awakening.
Set the mind, body,
and soul free, and
be awakened
spiritually."

Quotation #71

"*Spirituality* is a
gift from the
spiritual *soul*.
Accept the gift and
be *awakened*."

Quotation #72

"*Wrap* the gift of the *present* with *love* and care as you send *her* off to the *future*, for *know* this, the future, a *stranger*, accepts your *gift* without *saying* a *word*."

Quotation #73

"*The* future *knocks* on all doors as the *gift* of the *present* is but over. As *you* open the doors to the *future*, do carry the *blessings* of the *present* and the past with *you* on your *journey*."

Quotation #74

"*Victory* from a *journey*, through *mind* to mind is but possible *with* efforts placed *in* union upon a *plate* of *goals*."

Quotation #75

"*Each* sacred mind is the *beholder* of the *sacred* pot of gold. Placed together *in union*, we have the sacred *mountain* of gold in front of *us*."

Quotation #76

"*Worshipping* the path *to* victory, not *the* worshipped, leads all to *victory*."

Quotation #77

"*Do* not let your path choose your *destiny*, but *let* destiny choose your *path*."

Quotation #78

"*Do* not open the door by force. *Wait* until the door but *opens* for *then* the path is *made*."

Quotation #79

"*God* is found in all creation for *all* are but the *creation* of The *Creator.*"

Quotation #80

"*The* Creator
never left us for within
The Heavens, the
Earth, and amidst all
of the creation,
The Creator but is.
Find yourself first,
then find all the love
within this universe,
for then you will find
The *Creator.*"

Quotation #81

"*The* wise, the *unwise*, all are on this *journey* of life *searching* for wisdom. *Life* continues with *or* without *us*, so *wisdom* must still not be *found*."

Quotation #82

"*The* Creator but created one *family* with *different* color, race, *and* religion for it is *then* no one on Earth is *but* without a family *or* is but an *orphan*."

Quotation #83

"*The* Creator has placed no *walls amongst* all creation as *Mother* Earth is *one* house with no *walls*. Why is it *then* we the *creation* but have created a *wall*?"

"*Open* up and accept the differences *all* around you and *then* *realize* you have but *created* the most amazing *rainbow*."

Quotation #85

"*Religion* is the freedom *of* the *beholder*, not of the *captive*."

Quotation #86

"*Build* your faith *within* your soul and let *your* soul be your *guide*. Do not let *the* guide be your *soul*."

Quotation #87

"*Do* not keep your religion *captive*, but set it free *for* all and *may* the blessings *and* protection *awaken* all spiritual *souls*."

Quotation #88

"*The* door of repentance is *found* as the *soul* but has *awakened*."

Quotation #89

"*The* Creator sets free all of the *creation*. As we *wander* around frail and *tired*, *we* eventually *return* home to our *nest*, where *The* Creator awaits with open *arms*."

Quotation #90

"*The* love between
The Creator *and* the
creation *lives*
beyond *eternity*."

Quotation #91

"*The* sun, the moon, and the stars, *The Heavens* above and *Earth* beyond, all but *know* the *complete* truth. If only we *could* but hear *them*."

Quotation #92

"*Listen* to the truth.
Do not be lost *trying*
to find it, for *then*
only *you* shall
be *heard*."

Quotation #93

"*Do* not walk away from the inner *peace*. *Wandering* around for *eternity* to find peace, *you* shall be but *lost*. Find the inner peace *within* you. It is *then*, peace shall be *found*."

Quotation #94

"*Captivate* all with words of *truth* and just, not *through* lies and deceit *for* then it is *you* who shall be *caught*."

Quotation #95

"*Set* yourself free from the burden *of* this world as you *realize* no one is *but* a burden for all *belong* to The *Creator*."

Quotation #96

"*As* the sun sets on one *door*, he but awakens *at* another. Never lose *hope for* he shall be *back* as dawn breaks *open*."

Quotation #97

"*From* dawn to dusk,
all is but *lighted* up.
From dusk to dawn,
all is but left in
the dark. It is then oh
the creation *become*
the *hope* of light
for *all*."

Quotation #98

"*Even* when all is but lost *and* nothing is but right, even *then*, know the guiding *lights* are *always* there, *shining* hope *throughout* the dark night's *sky*."

Quotation #99

"Forever yours, with this *oath The* Creator and the creation are *but."*

Quotation #100

"*Blessed* heart beats The *Creator's* name as *she* but *awakens* through this *journey* of *life.*"

Quotation #101

"*Spiritual awakening* is the eternal *blessing* given to us *by* the awakened *soul*."

Quotation #102

"*Time* is a
never-ending *game*.
Do not run *after*
it, for *it* is always
ahead of *you*.
Learn to *live* within
it, for *then* she
belongs to you as
you belong to *her*."

Quotation #103

"*Heal* all through the
sweet songs of life,
for the *songs*
are but *heard* as
the *stories* are
but *written*."

Quotation #104

"*Songs* are the sweetest *heartbeats* of life. In times of *joy* or *sorrow*, we end up *clinging* to these *songs* of life for *comfort*."

Quotation #105

"*Complete* the *stories* of life through the *future* from the *past*. For when the *present* is but the *future*, the *stories* are but *complete*."

Quotation #106

"*Complete*
knowledge is the *gift*
of the *future* which is
always in
the future for
the *future*."

Quotation #107

"*Satisfaction* is but the complete *journey* of the *satisfied*, if the *trip* has been *made* through *satisfaction*."

Quotation #108

"*The* journey of love unites the *ocean*, the lands, and *all* on her way, for in *love* there is no *pick* and choose, but *all inclusive*."

"*Blessed* be the *Mother* and blessed be the *Father* who but *hold* all children and *know* this *child* is but a *gift* from The *Creator*."

Quotation #110

"*Love* forever is but the *eternal* blessings of *eternity*. Live *forever* through *love*."

Quotation #111

"*If* life is a choice between *blessings*, forgiveness, *mercy*, and *love*, I choose all of the *above*, but then I *know* I must *give* up something, so I give up *anger*."

Quotation #112

"*Dreams* are *blessings* from within the *soul*. Make them into *reality* as you *travel* through the *journey* of *life*."

Quotation #113

"*Life* is a journey throughout *time* where I *chose* my *Creator* as my *Guide*."

Quotation #114

"*The* lighthouse, the keeper, *and* the time *traveler* all *unite* for the ocean of *life.*"

Quotation #115

"*The* sailors, the passengers, *and* the ferry boats all *cross* the ocean of *sin* with The Creator's *name* on their *lips*."

Quotation #116

"*Holding* on to the boats of *hope*, all but cross the *ocean* of sin, *repenting* along the *way*."

Quotation #117

"*Obstacles* summon up the *courage* from within to *fight* for oneself and *teach* all others along the *way.*"

Quotation #118

"*Live* life with courage
to fight for the *truth*,
for when *and* where
truth is but *found*,
life is but *lived*."

Quotation #119

"*I* will spread peace *even* if I am standing *alone* against the *windstorm.*"

Quotation #120

"*Words* placed on *paper* become history as *words* placed in the *air* get lost in *history*."

Quotation #121

"*Even* when all is but lost in history, *life* is a *dream* lived *through* the *dreamer*."

Quotation #122

"*All* but ends as
windstorms come
and remove all the
pages out of history.
Even then, memories
storm back
throughout
time as she creates
new histories as all
but begins *again*."

"*All* that ends but *begins* again, as one *love* story ends, *another* one begins."

Quotation #124

"*Love* stories cross the bridges of *death* as they conquer *life and* death throughout *eternity.*"

Quotation #125

"*Life* is a blessed love *story* which had *begun* as the creation *were* but *created* by The Beloved *Creator.*"

Quotation #126

"*The* sun sets
as all are but *left* in the
dark. It is now
throughout the
darkness, we
must learn to *live* and
survive as we fight
for the *sun* to
but *rise*."

Quotation #127

"*Wind* whispers all throughout the *dark* nights as she *warns* all to *know* the *difference* between the *good* and the *evil*."

Quotation #128

"*The* good and the evil *live* within the soul. *Know* the *difference* as you fight and *awaken* *spiritually.*"

Quotation #129

"*Spiritual* awakening rejuvenates the *soul* as she *repents*, *redeems*, and *awakens*."

Quotation #130

"*The* repented, the *redeemed*, and the awakened *await* the *blessings* of eternal *peace* as they travel through *life*."

Quotation #131

"*Spiritual* awakening has no *walls* of religion, *but* has *complete* freedom of the *soul*."

Quotation #132

"*My* spiritual *awakening* landed me upon this *journey* of *life* where a *cleansing* of the *soul* started as I woke up *first*."

Quotation #133

"*The* Creator and the creation are *bound* to no *walls*, but complete *faith* within each *other*."

Quotation #134

"*Faith* is a complete *sacred*, spiritual journey *of* life. *Travel* upon it to believe *it*."

Quotation #135

"*The* believer is the *beholder* of the complete *truth*. Once *acquired*, the *journey* is but *complete*."

Quotation #136

"*The* moon shines upon the *lands* as nightfall but *begins*. *Warnings* she gives all, *beware for* darkness but *begins*."

Quotation #137

"*The* Earth, the ocean, and the sky *live* on *forever*. Its *inhabitants* but *change*."

Quotation #138

"*What* is no more cannot guide *you* to more, so *always* *find* what is, not what *was*."

Quotation #139

"*What* is but lost is the *past*. What is but to be *found* is the future. Do not *live* in the past *or* the future, but *let* the present be your *guide* for is the *present* also not known as a *gift*?"

Quotation #140

"*Life* is about making the correct *decision*. *Do* not let the decisions *make* you. *You* make the *decision*."

Quotation #141

ABOUT THE AUTHOR

I am an unknown person who lived the struggles, overcame the obstacles, as I have endured the pain and joy of life as they landed upon my door.

I like to be the unknown face to whom all can relate. I want you to see your face in the mirror when you search for me, not mine. For if it is my face in the mirror, then my friend you see a stranger. The unknown face is there so you see only yourself, your struggles, your achievements as you cross the journey of life. I want to be the face of a white, black, and brown, as well as the love we are always searching eternally for. If this world would have allowed, I would have distributed this inspirational quotation book to you with my own hands as a gift from a friend. Please take this book as a message from a friend.

You have my name and know I will always be there for anyone who seeks me. You can follow me @AnnahMariahRuby on Twitter, Ann Marie on my personal Facebook profile where the username is /annah.mariah.735, @TheAnnMarieRuby on my Facebook page, ann_marie_ruby on Instagram, and @TheAnnMarieRuby on Pinterest.

For more information about any one of my books, please visit my website www.annmarieruby.com.

I have published four books of original inspirational quotations:

> *Spiritual Travelers: Life's Journey From The Past To The Present For The Future*

Spiritual Messages: From A Bottle

Spiritual Journey: Life's Eternal Blessings

Spiritual Inspirations: Sacred Words Of Wisdom

For all of you whom have requested my complete inspirational quotations, now I have for all of you, my complete ark of inspiration, I but call:

Spiritual Ark: The Enchanted Journey Of Timeless Quotations.

I have also published a book of original prayers:

Spiritual Songs: Letters From My Chest.

I am blessed to also share with you information about my upcoming book:

Spiritual Lighthouse: The Dream Diaries Of Ann Marie Ruby.

I give a sample from my prayer book, *Spiritual Songs: Letters From My Chest* as I have written this book of prayers from my heart for all of whom seek the spiritual journey.

FOREVER YOURS
MY LORD

My Lord, forgive the sins.

My Lord, accept the repentance.

My Lord, give us Your protection.

My Lord, give us the direction.

We ask my Lord and we seek and we knock.

My Lord answer.

My Lord answer.

My Lord answer.

Until my last breath,

I shall call upon You, my Lord.

All the strength, all the might,

And all the powers cannot keep me away

From You, my Lord.

The only thing that shall make this body stop

Calling upon You, my Lord, is my last breath

For as I leave this body, I shall still be

Yours my Lord.

For I take the vow,

This mind, body, and soul belong only to You.

My Lord, give me courage.

Give me wisdom.

Show me the path.

Show me the way, so I may be on

Your blessed journey.

For every breath I take is

For You in Your name my Lord.

Every heartbeat that keeps me going is

For You, my Lord.

The day, the time, that but shall arrive

When all of Your creation will be no more,

May this creation be Yours even in death.

For a bond between the parents and child

Never breaks even in death.

This creation belongs only to You, my Lord.

For I raise my hands in salutation,

I prostrate only to You,

And I worship only You.

For my mind, body, and soul

Belong only to my Lord.

For I am Your creation

Who awaits upon Your Path,

Hands held up high in salutation,

Mind, body, and soul in prostration,

Counting each day and each night

For I know the time comes upon me.

My Lord, my Lord, my Lord,

As the time ends when all of this shall be no more,

Even then, may this creation always be

Forever Yours my Lord.

May I be Forever Yours my Lord.

FOREVER YOURS
MY LORD.

*From my prayer book, *Spiritual Songs: Letters From My Chest*.

My Spiritual Collection

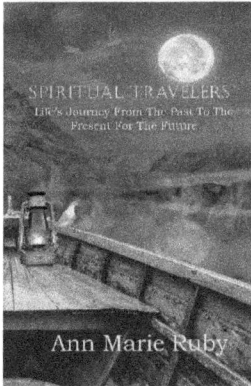

Spiritual Travelers:
Life's Journey From
The Past To The Present
For The Future

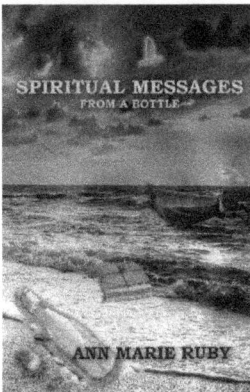

Spiritual Messages:
From A Bottle

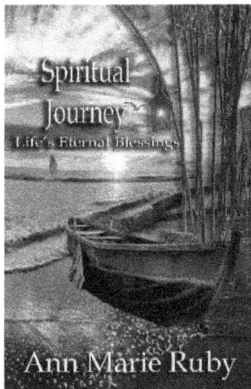

Spiritual Journey:
Life's Eternal Blessings

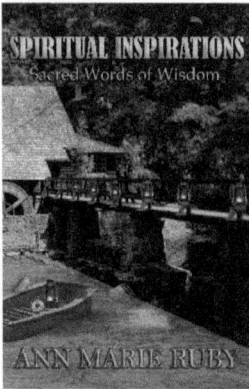

Spiritual Inspirations:
Sacred Words Of
Wisdom

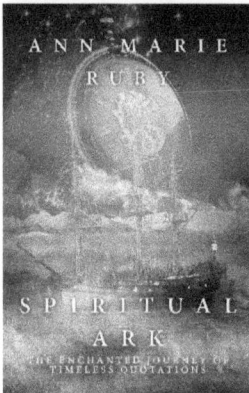

Spiritual Ark:
The Enchanted
Journey Of Timeless
Quotations

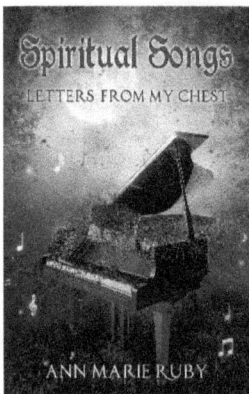

Spiritual Songs:
Letters From My Chest

My Upcoming Book

Spiritual Lighthouse:
The Dream Diaries Of Ann Marie Ruby

Within the dark, starless, foggy nights, my dreams appeared like the lighthouse always guiding me throughout my life. Dreams are spiritual guidance from the unknown. When the human body but falls asleep, it is then that our spiritual soul guides us throughout eternity. The soul walks into a parallel world where the past and the future exist in the same universe. Walk with me, as my soul but has walked the past and the future all throughout my life. Warnings, dangers, and surprises came upon my door, always guiding me like a lighthouse blinking in the dark night's sky. Alone, lost, and stranded I was until a lighthouse appeared within the ocean of the lost, my blessed dreams.

Take my hands and walk with me along this very personal path, as we journey together through my dream diaries, I call her, *Spiritual Lighthouse: The Dream Diaries Of Ann Marie Ruby*.

"Dreams are given from the Heavens above onto all within the Earth beneath for within them lie the miracles of eternity.

www.ingramcontent.com/pod-product-compliance
Lightning Source LLC
Chambersburg PA
CBHW021342290326
41933CB00037B/341